D0987097

M

J DAV
Davidson, Margaret
Seven true horse stories

A65500 399589

Seven True Horse Stories

Seven True Horse Stories

by Margaret Davidson

Illustrated by Leo Summers

with Sonia O. Lisker

65797

HASTINGS HOUSE
Publishers
New York 10016

Especially for
Julie, Brian, and Adam

Text copyright © 1979 by Margaret Davidson. Illustrations pages 1, 2, 16, 22, 27, 28–29, 32, 38–39, 43, 51, 54, 63, 78, 80, 86 by Leo Summers, copyright © 1979 by Scholastic Magazines. Illustrations pages 6, 67, 74 by Sonia O. Lisker, copyright © 1979 by Hastings House. This edition is published by Hastings House by arrangement with Scholastic Book Services, a division of Scholastic Magazines, Inc. All rights reserved. No part of this publication may be reproduced, stored in a retrieval system, or transmitted, in any form or by any means, electronic, mechanical, photocopying, recording or otherwise, without the prior permission of the copyright owner or the publishers.

Library of Congress Cataloging in Publication Data

Davidson, Margaret
   Seven true horse stories.
   Bibliography: p.
   Includes index.
   SUMMARY: An anthology of seven horse stories including the saga of a famous Chincoteague pony and Justin Morgan's big little horse.
   1. Horses — Legends and stories. 2. Horses — Juvenile literature. [1. Horses] I. Summers, Leo. II. Title.
SF302. D38   636.1   78-21149
ISBN 0-8038-6760-3

Published simultaneously in Canada by Saunders of Toronto, Ltd., Don Mills, Ontario
Printed in the United States of America

Contents

THE STORY OF EOHIPPUS
the horse that started it all

It was about as big as a fox. Its body was higher in back than in front, so it looked a little like a rabbit. It had paws with toes, like a dog. When it ran it bounced up and down like a pig. And its brain was very simple — about as simple as a bird's, most scientists think.

Its name was EOHIPPUS. EO means *dawn*. HIPPUS means *horse*. So these odd little animals who once lived in many places of the world were the first known ancestors of the horse.

These first horses looked like nothing

alive today. Yet they managed to live very well. Their world was different too.

Sixty million years ago the weather was hot almost everywhere — even in winter. Vine-choked jungles and forests covered much of the land. Crocodiles and giant lizards and other strange creatures slithered through muddy marshes and swamps. And many of these big, fierce animals were very eager to turn Eohippus into their next meal. Yet more often than not those first little horses managed to escape.

The dawn horse couldn't see very well because its eyes were too small. But it didn't have to see long distances. It could *hear* a bigger animal as it came crashing through the underbrush.

Eohippus couldn't run very fast either. Its legs were too short, so it hid from its enemies instead. When a hungry animal got too close, the dawn horse simply slipped behind a nearby rock or tree.

Its teeth were soft and small. But the

food it nibbled — seeds and fruit and tender leaves from trees — was easy to chew. And its many-toed paws were perfect for padding along a leafy forest trail. No wonder Eohippus lived very well in its wet, warm world.

But then the world began to change. Little by little the weather was growing cooler and drier. Many of the forests disappeared. The swamps dried up. Great empty fields of grass took their places. And still horses managed to survive — for they were changing too.

Of course those early horses couldn't change their own bodies — not in one lifetime. No animal can do that. But they had children — and a few of these children were just a little different. Some of these small changes helped keep horses alive.

A few horses happened to be born with brains just a bit bigger and more complex than before. Because they were smarter, they could solve the problems they faced more easily. Problems like how to find enough food to eat — and how to keep from being eaten by other animals while they did.

So more of these bigger-brained horses grew up to have children of their own — and most of these children were bigger-brained too.

What happened to the ones who didn't change — the horses who stayed smaller-brained? More of them starved — and more were eaten. So after many, many generations all horses had bigger, better brains.

Successful horses changed in other ways too. Their eyes grew bigger — so they could see an enemy while it was still far away. Their legs grew longer — so they could run for their lives when they had to.

Paws had been perfect for padding through a jungle or across a muddy swamp. But after a while most of the places horses lived were hard and dry. So their side toes grew smaller while their middle toes got bigger. Finally horses were standing on four hard hoofs instead of paws.

All these changes helped keep them safe. But horses had to eat too. Eohippus had plenty of soft things to nibble on. But as time passed horses had only one thing to eat — grass.

Grass looks soft enough. But try to chew a blade of it. You can chew and chew and it will hardly soften up at all. If *we* had to eat grass every day, scientists say, our teeth would wear right down to the gums in less than two years!

So after a while horses with small, soft teeth died. Then only the grazers were left — horses with great big teeth as hard as cement.

All this changing took a long, long time — millions and millions of years. But finally about 10,000 years ago a horse developed in the western part of America that looked very, very different from Eohippus — the little dawn horse that had started it all.

This animal was tall and long-legged. Its teeth were big and strong. Its hoofs were hard. Its brain and muscles were highly developed. This was Equus — the same horse we know today.

But what about all the earlier horses that had lived in other places of the world? They had not been able to change enough to fit the world they happened to be living in. So they died. Now only Equus was left. And the only place it lived was North America. That's why scientists say America is the true home of the horse.

But horses love to wander. Before long Equus roamed down into South America. It also drifted north to Alaska. And then it wandered farther west to Asia.

Today this would be impossible — for there's nothing between Alaska and Asia except water. But once the seas were much lower. They were so shallow that a narrow bridge of land tied the two places together. Before long, horses began drifting across this bridge to roam in the faraway places beyond.

It was a good thing they did. For about 5,000 years ago something very mysterious began to happen to the horses that had stayed behind in America. They all began to die!

No one knows why to this day. Some scientists think that Indians ate them

all. But Indians ate deer and buffalo too — and these animals managed to survive.

Some scientists think that the weather grew too cold. But horses had lived during colder times.

Some scientists think horses ran out of grass to eat. But there was plenty left over for other grazing animals, like deer and goats.

And many scientists think that the horses in America all died of some strange disease — a kind of sleeping sickness carried by mosquitos.

But the mystery has never been solved. Scientists are really sure of only one thing. Equus did disappear from the only place that had been its home from the very first.

Luckily those horses that crossed the land bridge to Asia didn't die — they multiplied. As time passed great herds spread all across Asia — and into Africa and Europe as well.

At first the people who lived in these

places could think of only one thing to do with horses — eat them. But before long they began to realize that horses were much more useful alive. They helped farmers farm. They hauled heavy loads. They took people from place to place. They even carried men to war. "Next to God," one soldier wrote his king, "we owe our victory to the horses!"

But all this while there was one place where no horses roamed. America. Then in the early 1500's Spanish explorers began arriving — looking for silver and gold. They brought a few horses with them. Before long other people began coming. And they brought horses too.

It had taken a long, long time. But the round-the-world trip was over at last. Once more Equus grazed across the land where it had first lived.

The horse was home again.

THE STORY OF JUSTIN MORGAN

the biggest little horse of all

Justin Morgan walked along a dirt road in Massachusetts. He was too poor to own a horse. This was two hundred years ago, so he had to walk wherever he wanted to go. Justin had come all the way from Vermont to collect some money a man owed him.

But when he got there the man said, "If you want money you'll just have to wait. I can give you something else though." He pointed to two horses in a field nearby.

Justin was a teacher. He didn't need a horse. And the man owed him much more money than Justin would get from selling those two horses. But he had come a long way. Two horses were better than nothing. Finally Justin nodded and started home with the horses.

One horse was big and powerful-looking. Justin could sell him. But he shook his head when he looked at the other horse — a colt he named Figure. Figure was only fourteen hands high (a hand is four inches). That wasn't very big for a horse. "He's probably worth nothing at all," Justin thought.

Figure had run wild for two years. His coat was covered with mud and dust. Justin could hardly tell what color he was. So when he reached home, Justin Morgan washed the little horse. He picked all the burrs out of his mane and tail. Then he brushed and combed him all over until the horse's coat gleamed in the sun.

"Why, he's *handsome!*" Justin's daughter Emily cried.

It was true. The horse's legs and

ears were a shiny black. The rest of his coat was a nice reddish-brown. His mane and tail were thick and long. His back was straight and his muscles firm and strong.

Figure had never been trained. But he learned quickly. Soon he was pulling carriages and wagons. He was so gentle that the youngest child could ride him.

And he was smart. "Sometimes I think that horse knows what I'm thinking before I do myself," Justin said.

Figure was strong too. He could carry a rider or pull a wagon all day — and never seem to tire. Best of all, he was always willing to do whatever was asked of him.

Justin Morgan was proud of Figure. But he was very poor. He couldn't afford to keep a horse. He didn't want to sell him either. Maybe he could rent him to someone.

Justin went to a neighbor named Robert Evans. "I hear you need a horse," he said. "What about renting mine?"

Mr. Evans had heard good things about Figure, but still he said, "That horse of yours is too small — and the work I do is mighty hard. What I need is a really *big* horse."

Justin smiled and said, "Try him." So for fifteen dollars a year Figure was rented to Robert Evans. Soon Mr. Evans knew just how good a bargain he'd made.

Two hundred years ago horses did the work that farm machines and cars do today. They were never treated like pets. They were work animals — that was all.

Every day Evans and Figure went to work. From dawn to dark they hauled heavy logs out of the woods. They pulled big stumps and rocks from the ground. It was hard, hard work — but Figure was always willing.

One evening Robert Evans and Figure passed a sawmill on their way home. Men and horses were standing in the clearing in front of the mill. A huge pine log lay on the ground — more than 150 feet from the sawmill.

"What's going on?" Robert Evans called out. A man explained. One horse after another had tried to drag the log to the mill. But none had been able to move it more than a few inches.

Robert Evans walked over to the log. He looked at it from one side — and then the other. "Why, Figure can do it," he said. Everyone looked at Justin Morgan's horse. Some began to laugh. "*That* horse?" one man said. "Why, horses almost twice his size couldn't move that log."

"I say Figure can do it," he said again. "And I say he can do it in three pulls — or less."

He snapped one end of a heavy chain to Figure's harness. He wrapped the other end around the log. Then he patted Figure on the shoulder. "All right, boy," he said quietly. "It's just another log — only bigger."

Then "Giddap!" he cried. Figure tensed. He leaned forward. His hoofs dug into the ground. Every muscle in his body strained. He was pulling as hard as he could. And nothing was happening.

Then somehow he pulled just a little bit harder — and the log moved! At first only an inch. Then three inches.

Then a foot! Slowly Figure dragged the log to the middle of the clearing.

"Whoa, boy," Robert Evans said. For a few minutes the little horse rested. Then "Come on," said Robert Evans. "Time to work some more."

Once more Figure strained forward. Once more the log began to move slowly and steadily — right up to the mill.

Everyone began to talk at once. "What a horse," one man said. "Why, that Morgan horse is the *biggest* little horse I ever saw!"

A few weeks later — at the end of a hard day's work — Robert Evans and Figure passed a country store where a group of men were racing their horses.

"Want to try your horse, Evans?" someone called.

Robert Evans nodded. "I might."

"Oh, come on," one of the men said. "I know Morgan's horse can pull logs. But his legs are too short for racing."

"I'm sure he can do as well as the next one," Evans said. "I think I'd like to try."

Figure had never been in a race. Still, he seemed to sense that something exciting was about to happen. He began to prance. Then — "One-two-three . . . Go!" someone shouted.

Figure took the lead right away! The race wasn't over, though. The other horses had much longer legs. Surely they would catch up before he got to the end. But Figure held his lead. He won by four times the length of his own body.

Figure ran in many races after that, and he won most of them too. Even thoroughbreds — horses specially bred for speed — were usually no match for the tough little Morgan horse.

One day Justin Morgan went to see Robert Evans. "I need money badly," he said. "The fifteen dollars rent you pay for Figure each year is just not enough. I hate to do it — but I have to sell the horse." So both men watched sadly as Figure was led away.

Soon after that Justin Morgan became sick. His fever rose and his cough grew worse and worse. One day he lay in bed talking to a friend. "I know I am dying," he said. "And soon no one will know I've been alive. No one will remember my name."

How wrong he was! Already many people were calling Figure by Justin Morgan's name. Before long everyone would be thinking of the *horse* as Justin Morgan.

People talked about the horse Justin Morgan because they had noticed something very unusual. The children of Justin Morgan all looked like him. It didn't matter what the foal's mother looked like. They all had his same intelligent eyes. They all had his sturdy legs and strong muscles. And his children grew up to *be* like him too. They were all gentle yet spirited, strong and fast and eager to work.

People wanted horses with these qualities. So they mated their own horses to the first Justin Morgan and then to his children and grandchildren and great-grandchildren.

Soon Morgan horses were carrying the mail. They were taking Americans westward — all the way to California. They were fighting in wars and working on farms. They became fire horses and police horses and racing horses and riding horses. Thousands of Morgan horses did all these things and more — as they helped build the United States of America.

And today, in Justin Morgan's home state of Vermont, there is a special farm just for breeding and raising Morgan horses. In front of the biggest barn on the farm there is a big bronze statue of Justin Morgan — the father of the first truly American breed of horse.

65797

THE STORY OF THE PACING WHITE MUSTANG

the horse no one could tame

ILLINOIS PRAIRIE DISTRICT LIBRARY

Mustangs — the wild horses of the American prairie — are usually small and tough-looking. But the Pacing White Mustang was tall and fine-boned. His thick mane hung down to his knees. And his tail swished against the ground as he grazed across the grasslands of central Texas.

One thing more set him apart from the other wild horses. From the tips of his ears to the end of that long tail he was pure white.

He was a natural leader too. Most stallions had a family of about fifteen

or twenty mares. That was all they could control. But the Pacing White Mustang led more than fifty!

It wasn't easy to keep such a family safe. There were always other stallions waiting nearby to steal his mares away.

Men meant danger too. Many of them wanted to capture the big white horse. They wanted to capture him and tame the wildness out of him forever.

But the stallion was too smart to be trapped. And he paced too fast to be caught. (Pacing is a special, very smooth way of running. Most horses gallop when they want to go fast.)

Over the years, one cowboy after another tried to trap the Pacing White Mustang or chase him down. Stories of his escapes were told in bunkhouses all over the Southwest.

One morning a cowboy rode by. The Mustang noticed him. But he was still far away, so the horse went on grazing. Suddenly the cowboy whirled. Now he was racing straight for the Mustang!

The big white horse knew just what to do. He circled round and round his mares and foals, crowding them together into a tight bunch. Then he began pacing south, with his family close behind.

The Mustang paced steadily for hours. He wasn't tired. But toward the end of the day he began to move more slowly. He was sure he was safe. No horse and rider had ever followed him this far before.

He glanced back, just to make sure. And for a moment his smooth pace broke. He was still being chased!

One man had never been able to run the wild horse down. And people knew that the stallion always headed south when he was chased. So they made a plan. One cowboy would ride behind him for about thirty miles. Then he would meet a second cowboy who had been sent ahead to wait. This man would ride on until he came to where a third man was waiting — fresh and ready to pick up the chase.

There were twelve men and horses in all — twelve links in a chain stretching south for hundreds of miles. Surely not even the Pacing White Mustang could escape them all!

One thing was certain. He was going to try. Soon the sun would go down. Always before the Mustang had been able to escape at night. He was a wild creature of the prairies, and he moved fast in the dark. Most of the ranch-bred horses that chased him weren't sure-footed enough to do that.

But the men who were chasing him had planned well. As the sun sank, a full moon rose to take its place in the sky. Its warm yellow glow lit the prairie for miles around.

All through the night the Mustang paced ahead of his enemies. "He looked like a ship," one of the men said later. "A ghostly white ship sailing through a sea of grass."

As the sun rose next morning the Mustang looked back. A horse and rider were still there! Would he *ever* lose this terrible enemy who never seemed to tire?

For many miles the Mustang's family had been able to keep up with him. But one by one they had tired and dropped behind — first the foals and then the mares. Now he was running alone.

His eyes were glazed. His white coat was caked with dust. His chest heaved painfully with every breath he took. Even his great strength was finally fading. Still something in him cried *keep moving*.

On and on he paced until, by the edge of the Frio River in South Texas, the last cowboy gave up the chase. He pulled up and watched as the Mustang swam to the other side and paced out of sight. "The last thing I saw was that white tail of his waving good-bye," he said later.

No one was chasing him now. But still the Mustang kept moving south.

Every few miles he stopped to eat a
few mouthfuls of grass and sniff the air
for danger. Then he would start pacing
slowly again. He was almost to the
Mexican border when he stopped once
more. He lifted his head and took a
deep sniff of air. He smelled no
danger. He did smell something else
though. Water!

The big horse snorted with pleasure.
Quickly he followed the smell of water
into a nearby canyon.

The Pacing White Mustang had not
smelled an enemy. But a cowboy from
a nearby ranch had seen him. The
cowboy slipped behind some tall
bushes. The wind was blowing his special human smell *away* from the horse.

The cowboy had never seen the Pacing White Mustang. But he had heard
of him many times. "Yes!" he thought
as he looked at the beautiful animal.
"It's the White Mustang!" And the
cowboy smiled — for he knew that

when a horse is full of water, he can't run very fast.

At last the stallion came out of the canyon. Quickly the man whirled his long lasso into the air. It sailed toward the exhausted horse — and the noose settled around his powerful neck!

The Pacing White Mustang screamed with fury. He reared and bucked and hurled himself away from the lasso. He pawed the air with his hoofs. But he couldn't get rid of that terrible rope!

Suddenly he wheeled and ran straight toward the cowboy. The look in his eye was all too plain to read. But the cowboy was lucky. There was a tree nearby. Somehow he got behind it. He kept the tree between himself and the furious stallion. And the tree served as a kind of hitching-post. Round and round its trunk the cowboy wrapped his end of the lasso. The Pacing White Mustang was caught!

The cowboy raced to his ranch and

came back with two other cowboys. They too tied ropes around the raging stallion. Then — screaming and fighting every foot of the way — he was dragged back to the ranch.

The cowboys wrestled him into a small fenced-in corral. And suddenly the horse stopped fighting. He seemed to know he had been beaten at last.

The men brought him a big bundle of grass and a barrel of well water. The horse turned his head. He would not eat or drink.

"He'll eat when he gets hungry enough," one of the cowboys said.

But for nine days and nights the Pacing White Mustang stood still as a statue. He never took a bite of the juicy grass. He never swallowed a drop of the sweet well water. And on the tenth morning he lay down on his side and died.

The horse who loved freedom so much had escaped after all.

THE STORY OF MISTY

the pony who helped
save a whole herd

It's Pony Penning Day!

Fishermen and chicken farmers who
live on the island of Chincoteague be-
come cowboys for a day. Early in the
morning they cross the narrow channel
of water that separates their island
from the neighboring island of Assateague.

There — more than five miles off the
coast of Virginia — live hundreds of
wild ponies. No one knows how the
little horses got there. But they have
roamed free on the island for hundreds
of years.

The cowboys round up the wild
ponies. They drive them into the water
and across the channel to Chincoteague. Then the whole herd — almost
two hundred stallions and mares and
foals of all ages — gallops down the
main street of town to the fair-
grounds.

Each year thousands of people from
all over the United States come to
Chincoteague on this day late in July.
They come to play games and watch

horse races and go on all sorts of car-
nival rides. Most of all they come to
look at the wild ponies. And some also
come to buy one. Every year many of
the half-grown ponies are sold. The
rest are driven back to Assateague. (If
some of the ponies weren't sold every
year, there soon would be too many on
the island — and not enough food for
any of them to eat.)

Twenty-five thousand people went
to Pony Penning Day in the summer of
1946. One was a writer named Marguerite Henry. Pony Penning Day was
almost over when Mrs. Henry saw a
mare standing a little apart from the
other ponies. Lying by the mare's side
was a tiny foal.

The foal's eyes were bright brown
with long gold eyelashes. Around one
eye was a big gold patch. It made the
baby horse look like a happy clown!

Mrs. Henry knew she had to own
this foal. But the mare and foal had already been sold to a man who lived on

Chincoteague — a man everyone called Grandpa Beebe.

And Grandpa didn't want to sell the pony. "She's only a week old. That's far too young to leave her mother. Take another," he said.

But Marguerite Henry knew that *this* was the foal she had to have — and no other. "I *need* her," she begged. "I'm a writer. I want to build a book around an Assateague pony. And somehow I know it will be a better book if this pony is with me while I'm writing it."

"Well..." Grandpa Beebe scratched his ear. "If you let her stay here for a few months — until she's old enough to leave her mother..."

"Of course!" Marguerite Henry agreed quickly. Then she made Grandpa Beebe a promise. "When she's old enough to be a mother herself, I'll send her back to you. Then her babies will be real Assateague ponies too."

Marguerite Henry went home and began to write her book — and a few months later the half-grown pony arrived in Illinois. Mrs. Henry named her Misty.

A few neighborhood children came to play with Misty. But no one else knew about the little horse who had come from so far away.

Then the book was finished. It was called *Misty of Chincoteague* — and from the beginning it was a huge success. The book was full of adventures — some of them true and some made up.

Now many people knew about Misty. Everyone wanted the little pony to pay them a visit. She was asked to horse shows. She visited schools and libraries and book stores. She went to all kinds of parties. Finally Marguerite Henry had to buy a special notebook — just to write down all of Misty's invitations!

Misty loved those trips. She liked to

show off. And she had learned some tricks. She had a little blue stool. She learned to put her front hoofs up on it and bow from left to right. She also learned to shake "hands" with her right or left hoof. Soon she was offering a hoof to almost everyone in sight!

Marguerite Henry had made a prom-

ise to Grandpa Beebe. She had promised to send Misty back to Chincoteague when she was old enough to be a mother. But Mrs. Henry loved Misty so! Somehow the years kept slipping by — and Misty was still in Illinois.

Finally Mrs. Henry knew it was time — no, it was past time — to send Misty back to her first home. "Don't worry," she said to the many children who came to say good-bye. "I *know* Misty will be happy in her new home."

And she was. Misty spent her days running through the pine woods and salty meadows with Grandpa Beebe's other ponies. And about a year later her first baby was born. All across the country, radio and television stations carried the good news about the new mother and her little colt named Phantom Wings.

Anyone who had not heard of Misty before soon found out who she was. A movie was made of the book *Misty of*

Chincoteague. Misty didn't play herself in the movie, of course. It was about a very young pony and Misty was full grown now. But she played one of the wild horses in the crowd scenes. When she wasn't acting she spent a lot of time shaking hands with anyone who happened to be nearby.

Then it was the spring of 1962. Early one morning heavy clouds rolled across the sky. The day grew darker and darker. An icy cold wind blew from the north. By evening a freezing rain was falling.

Most people weren't worried at first — they were used to stormy weather. But all night long the wind and rain grew worse. Early next morning the people of Chincoteague looked out their windows — and saw water everywhere! It was beginning to lap against the sides of their homes. And it was still rising!

Misty was about to have another baby. By midmorning water was flowing across the floor of her barn. The water was full of mud and sand and bits of strange things. First it slapped against her hoofs. Then inch by inch it started to creep up her legs. Misty gave a nervous whinny.

All day people sat by their radios and listened as the news grew worse. The causeway to the mainland was under water. The people of Chincoteague were cut off. They were trapped on a small piece of land five miles out in the raging sea!

Late in the afternoon the government said everyone would have to leave. Helicopters would take them to safe places on the mainland.

But what about Misty? There was no room in the helicopters for animals. The Beebes did the only thing they could. They led Misty across the watery back yard, up the porch steps, and into their kitchen. The house was on a small hill, so the floor was still dry. They piled hay in a corner and filled the big sink with water. They dumped all the vegetables in the refrigerator on the floor. Then they gave her one last pat and left.

The storm raged for four more days. Then the wind began to die. The rain stopped and the water began to go down. The causeway to the island was above water once more. The people of Chincoteague could go home.

But to what? The storm had done terrible damage. Some houses leaned crazily to one side. Others weren't there — they'd been swept out to sea. Cars and trucks had been tossed about like toys. Boats had been lifted out of the water and thrown high up on land.

But Misty was fine. She'd eaten all the hay and vegetables. She'd drunk all the water. Then — somehow — she had opened the refrigerator door and tipped over a full bottle of her favorite treat — molasses.

Early the next morning Misty gave birth to a little tan-and-white daughter.

It had been hard to name Misty's first baby. Everyone had a different idea. But there was no trouble naming this fuzzy little filly. She was Stormy, of course!

As soon as things had been cleaned up, a little group of men rowed over to Assateague. Some of the ponies there had reached higher land. But more than half the herd had been swept out to sea. Would there ever be another Pony Penning Day — with so few of the wild horses left?

Then someone had an idea. Suppose the people of Chincoteague bought back some of the ponies — those that had been sold in other years? These ponies would have foals and build up the herd once more. It was a good idea — but where would they get the money to buy the ponies?

Then one of the men who made the movie about Misty called the mayor of Chincoteague. He wanted to know how everyone was after the storm. The mayor told him about their problem.

"What if we show the movie again?" the man said. "We'll send it to every theater that wants it. And all the money it makes will go to help buy back the ponies."

It sounded wonderful. But so many children had just seen the movie. Would they go to see it again, so soon? What if Misty and Stormy went *with* the movie.... Surely the boys and girls would come then!

The first theater Misty and Stormy visited was in Richmond, Virginia. By ten o'clock the big theater was packed.

"We want Misty! We want Stormy!" the boys and girls yelled. A man came down the center aisle leading the two ponies. When they reached the steps to the stage, Misty trotted right up them. But Stormy stopped. Misty turned and whinnied softly. "Come along," she seemed to be saying. "*They're* nothing to be afraid of." Stormy stood for a moment more.

Then she wobbled up the steps too.

Misty's special blue stool was on the stage. As soon as she saw it she walked over and climbed up on it. Then she bowed from left to right. Everyone began to clap and whistle and yell. Misty looked back at the boys and girls and slowly blinked her eyes.

For three months mother and daughter went from town to town and theater to theater. Misty stood on her stool and shook hands with long lines of boys and girls. Stormy nursed and played happily on all the different stages. Sometimes mother and daughter stood nose to nose, making soft sounds to one another. As one man said when he saw them, "Those two are *born* actors!"

When the tour was over, enough money had been raised to buy back about fifty ponies. Misty and Stormy — along with boys and girls all across America — had saved the wild herd of Assateague!

THE STORY OF BRIGHTY

the donkey who
belonged to himself

"The buds are out on the aspens," Uncle Jim thought. "And yesterday I saw some ground squirrels. Brighty's sure to be coming up his trail any day now."

Brighty didn't belong to Uncle Jim Owens. He didn't belong to anyone — except himself. All donkeys are very independent, but Brighty was more independent than most.

Brighty wasn't a wild donkey. He wasn't tame either. No one knew where he came from. He spent half his winters in the Grand Canyon, where it was always warm. Sometimes while he was there, he helped an old miner by carrying his tools. But more often Brighty just played. He rolled on his back. He ran in the shallow creek, splashing water every which way. Often he sat and brayed at the top of his lungs.

Brighty always did just as he pleased. And now that spring had come, it pleased Brighty to climb the steep canyon to his cool summer home on the North Rim.

During the summer Brighty often visited Uncle Jim. But he didn't live with him. Brighty's special home was a cave near the edge of the canyon. The cave was always dim inside. Its floor was covered with soft ferns. And near the back wall was a deep pool of cool water.

One night as Brighty slept, a shape came creeping through the dark. It peered into the cave — and its eyes gleamed like gold.

It was a hungry mountain lion! For a moment the lion stood staring at Brighty. Then it crouched — and sprang! The lion was aiming to sink his claws into Brighty's neck — and that would have been the end of Brighty. But in the dark the lion missed. Not by much, but enough. Those terrible claws slashed down Brighty's front legs instead.

Brighty jumped to his feet. He kicked back hard with his little hoofs. But the lion leapt aside. Once more it crouched — and this time it sprang onto Brighty's back!

Brighty tore round and round the cave, trying to shake off that snarling cat. Then he fell to the ground and began rolling over and over. The lion didn't let go.

As Brighty rolled, he came closer

and closer to the pool. At last he rolled into the water — pinning the lion underneath him. The lion still fought wildly, trying to keep its head above water. But Brighty's body held it down. Two minutes, three minutes, then four minutes passed. Finally the cat's claws loosened. Brighty staggered out of the water and fell to the floor of the cave.

That's where Uncle Jim Owens found him the next day. He gasped as he stepped inside the cave. The dead lion lay in the pool. And Brighty was on his side, his eyes closed and his legs covered with blood.

Uncle Jim put his hand on Brighty's chest. The donkey's heart was still beating strongly. Quickly the man set to work. He gathered big gobs of gooey pine tar from a nearby tree and spread it all over Brighty's legs.

The soothing salve seemed to make Brighty feel better almost at once. He struggled to his knees. Swaying, he got to his feet. Then he began to do what any hurt animal does — he began to lick his wounds.

"You can't do that, fella," Uncle Jim said. "You'll take off all the pine tar." But Brighty just went on licking.

Uncle Jim sighed. If only he had some kind of bandage. Then Brighty wouldn't be able to get at the wounds.

Suddenly Uncle Jim had a crazy idea. He took out his pocketknife and cut off his left pant leg at the knee. Then he cut off the right one. He stepped out of the two pieces of cloth and pulled them up Brighty's front legs. The two bottom halves of Uncle Jim's pants covered Brighty right up to his chest.

But what could he use to keep the cloth up? Uncle Jim chuckled. He took off his bright-red suspenders and laid them across Brighty's back. Finally he clipped the suspenders to the tops of the cloth legs.

Now each of them — the man and

the donkey — was wearing half a pair of pants. "And pretty silly we look too!" Uncle Jim said.

Brighty lived at Uncle Jim Owens's ranch for the next few weeks. Every evening the old man slipped Brighty's pants off and rubbed his legs with soothing salve. Then he slipped the pants back on again.

One evening Uncle Jim came out of his house as usual. But he didn't collect any tar. Instead he pulled off Brighty's pants and threw them away. "You're all healed now," he told the donkey. "You don't need those pants anymore." Uncle Jim gave Brighty a slap on his rump. "So go on. You're free to go wherever you want now!"

Brighty dashed round and round in a big circle. And HEEEE-HAWWWW!— the sound of his happy bray filled the air.

But Brighty didn't leave the ranch. The summer days passed and he never even visited his cave. Soon it was fall.

Every day it grew colder on the high North Rim. It was long past time for Brighty to leave for his winter home deep in the Grand Canyon.

Often Brighty went to the edge of the canyon. He stood there for hours — staring down. But still he didn't leave.

Uncle Jim was getting more and more worried. He had healed Brighty's legs. Had he somehow tamed his free spirit too?

Then one day Brighty began to move down the trail — very, very slowly. As Uncle Jim watched, Brighty stopped and turned. He walked on a little more. And stopped again. Uncle Jim knew he could call, "Brighty, come back!" and the grateful animal would probably obey. But the man didn't make a sound. He just watched as Brighty moved down into the canyon. At last he was out of sight.

Uncle Jim would miss his friend. But he was happy all the same. For he knew that Brighty would remain a free donkey for the rest of his life.

So every winter Brighty lived deep in the canyon. Every summer he spent on the North Rim. And always he came and went the same way.

In those days — almost a hundred years ago — very few people tried to get down to the bottom of the Grand Canyon. Its sides were too steep and there were no trails. Little by little, Brighty's hoofs wore a path — a path people began calling Bright Angel Trail.

More and more people began to use Brighty's path — teachers and students and writers, miners and explorers and scientists. Many tourists came too. They all wanted to see what lay at the bottom of the Grand Canyon.

Sometimes Brighty stayed with these people for a while. When he felt like it he even worked for them. Often he gave children rides on his back. Sometimes three or four boys and girls would climb on at the same time. And Brighty would amble from place to place. When he got tired or bored he just walked under a low branch of a tree. It was his way of saying, "Time to get off now."

One morning in the winter of 1921 Brighty was awakened by a sound like thunder — only much louder. For a few minutes everything was quiet. Then the strange sound came again.

Brighty followed the sound to the bank of the Colorado River. There he blinked with surprise. Men were moving about everywhere. Suddenly the sound came once more. And big chunks of stone flew into the air. The men were dynamiting holes in the rock.

The Colorado River flows down the middle of the Grand Canyon. It is only four hundred feet wide. But it cuts the canyon in half. The men were building a bridge across the mighty river — a bridge to link the two halves of the canyon at last.

Brighty sat down to watch. "Hey! You must be Brighty," one of the workers called after a while. "Why don't you come help?"

Brighty walked over. And before long he was carrying tools and equipment. Often he carried heavy bags of sand for making cement. Brighty didn't work every day, of course. Just when he felt like it.

Slowly the bridge took shape. When it was finished many important people gathered for the Opening Day Ceremony. The Governor of Colorado made a fine speech. Then it was time for the first person to cross the bridge.

"I say Brighty should be the first one across," someone called out. "It's *his* trail that helped open up the canyon for the rest of us."

"Besides," another man added, "Brighty is the only true citizen of the Grand Canyon here today."

But *would* Brighty cross the bridge?

Donkeys don't like to do dangerous things. Certainly he would never go alone. Uncle Jim stepped forward. "I'll go with Brighty," he said.

They walked up to the bridge. At the edge, Brighty stopped in his tracks. The bridge was very long and narrow — and it was *swaying* in the wind.

Brighty's ears went back. He began to shake. Uncle Jim knew these signs well. Brighty was about to run away.

"Trust me, Brighty," Uncle Jim said quietly. "We'll be across in no time at all."

Uncle Jim put one of his own big feet on the bridge. He reached down and placed one of Brighty's tiny hoofs beside it. Brighty was still shaking. But he didn't bolt. Uncle Jim put his other foot on the bridge. He reached down again — and both Brighty's front hoofs were on the bridge too.

Now — with his hand on Brighty's shoulder — Uncle Jim began to walk.

And so did Brighty. Foot by foot they walked across the bridge until they were safe on the other side!

The men cheered wildly. *HEE-HAWWWWW!* Brighty brayed back.

Brighty's world was bigger now. He could wander on both sides of the Grand Canyon. But in the spring he always returned to his friends on the North Rim.

Then one spring Brighty didn't appear. He was never seen again. No one really knows what happened. Some people say Brighty was shot by an outlaw who was hiding in the canyon. But others say this isn't true. They say that Brighty lived a good long life in the Grand Canyon of Colorado. And finally he just died of old age. He died as he had lived — a free donkey to the last.

THE STORY OF RECKLESS
the horse Marine

Lieutenant Pedersen walked from stall to stall. Again and again he shook his head gloomily as he looked at the horses inside. Once these animals had all been sleek racehorses. But now they were painfully thin, and their coats were matted and dull. One was even covered with sores. The Korean War had been raging for two years now. And life had been hard for these horses.

Lieutenant Pedersen was the leader of a group of American Marines fighting in the war. He needed an animal to help carry ammunition to their guns. At first he had looked for a mule. But there were no mules to be found. So finally he had come to this race track.

He had almost decided he wasn't going to find an animal *here* either, when suddenly he saw her — a red filly with three white stockings and a long white blaze down the middle of her face. She too was painfully thin. But her eyes were bright and her coat was shiny. The Lieutenant held out his hand, and the horse walked right up to him.

"This is the one I want," he said.

A few hours later Lieutenant Pedersen and the horse arrived back in camp. The men came pouring out of their tents to see her.

"What are we going to call her, Lieutenant?" one of them asked.

Several Marines suggested names. Finally a soft southern voice said, "There's only one name we can give her."

"What's that?"

"Why, Reckless, of course."

The men belonged to a Marine Corps unit called the Recoilless Rifle Platoon. But most people called them the Reckless Rifles instead — for the big guns they served could be very dangerous to handle. So from then on the red racehorse was known by that name too.

At first the men worried about how they were going to feed Reckless. It wasn't going to be easy to find real horse food — hay and barley and oats. Not so close to the front lines.

But they soon discovered Reckless was willing to eat almost *anything*. Her favorite foods by far were cake and candy and Coca-Cola — which she liked to drink from a glass. The only food Reckless never learned to like was peanut butter. It stuck to the roof of her mouth.

Reckless was far too happy with her new friends to wander away. So the men let her roam freely. But sometimes at night she got lonely. Then she'd poke her head through the front

flap of a tent and whinny softly. "It's Reckless," someone would murmur sleepily. And the men would shove their cots out of the way to give her room to lie down too.

Reckless didn't spend all her time eating or visiting friends. She was also learning some important lessons from her trainer, Sergeant Joe Latham.

Sergeant Latham taught her to carry big rolls of wire on her back — wire for sending messages from one Marine unit to another. As she walked along, the wire unrolled on the ground behind her. Before long Reckless could lay wire much faster than any human Marine.

She learned to kneel and crawl into a fox-hole. She also learned to lie down quickly — for often during a battle enemy bullets whistled right by over-head.

Finally Joe Latham taught Reckless to carry shells for the guns. Each shell weighed twenty-four pounds. Reckless wasn't a big horse. But she turned out to be a tough one. She could carry six shells easily. She could carry ten if she had to. This was 240 pounds — more than a fourth of her own weight!

Sergeant Latham couldn't help bragging. "You tell her what you want," he said. "You let her look things over. Then if she's with someone she trusts, she'll find a way to do it."

But how would she act in a real battle? It was the winter of 1952 and a big battle was beginning nearby. "It's time to try Reckless out," Lieutenant Pedersen said.

First Sergeant Latham took Reckless to the ammunition area where she was loaded with shells. He led her forward to the front lines. Just then the first Recoilless Rifle was fired. *"Wham-whoossSSSH!"* The big gun made a terrible noise! Reckless jumped straight up in the air — shells and all. All four feet left the ground. When she came down her eyes were rolling and she was trembling with terror.

"Wham-whoosssSSSH!" A second gun was fired. Once more Reckless jumped — but not quite so far this time. It took her a while to get used to the guns. But finally she stopped trembling.

She worked steadily until the battle was almost over. Then one of the Marines happened to look at her. He burst out laughing. Someone had left a helmet lying on the ground, and Reckless was trying to eat the cloth lining out of it!

The men didn't say much after that battle. But they all knew that Reckless was truly one of them now — a Marine who had proved herself under fire.

Other battles followed — each one worse than the last. Finally the enemy took a hilly area known as Outpost Vegas. The next day orders were sent from Marine Corps Headquarters, *"Take back Outpost Vegas."*

The battle began at dawn. The noise was almost unbearable. Bombs and shells were exploding everywhere. Soon Sergeant Latham came to get Reckless.

She was standing by the back wall of her bunker. Her ears were flat against her head. It was a cool day but she was covered with sweat. Reckless had worked willingly for months now. But somehow she could tell that this battle was going to be different from all the others — different and more terrible.

Sergeant Latham held out a bucket of oats. Reckless turned away. For the first time she refused to eat. She wouldn't drink anything either. And when Sergeant Latham tried to lead her out of the bunker she dug in her hoofs.

"Come on, girl," the Sergeant said. "We *have* to go." Reckless stood still

for a moment more — then she followed her friend toward the ammunition area.

Shells were going to be needed des-
perately today. So from the first
Reckless was loaded with eight of
them — two more than usual. Then
one of the Marines led her toward the
guns. The way was long and dangerous.
First she had to cross a rice field. At
the end of the field was a steep, steep
hill. The Marine Corps guns were on
top of this hill — firing at the enemy
across a small valley. Reckless —
loaded down with shells — had to go
up this hill. All around bombs and
shells were exploding. Bullets whizzed
by. Bits of shrapnel filled the air.

She'd just been loaded for the sixth
trip when someone cried out, "Look at
Reckless!" She hadn't waited for anyone
to lead her this time. She had started
off on her own!

Half way across the rice field she
began to trot. Then she broke into a

gallop. As she started up the hill she was running as fast as she could — the shells bouncing up and down on her back. She just managed to make it to the top. The shells were unloaded while she caught her breath. Then she returned to the ammunition area again. Reckless had made the whole trip by herself! From then on she worked alone.

As time passed she lost most of her fear. Even when a bomb exploded a few feet away, she didn't look around. But she was so tired that she no longer ran up the hill. She crept up it.

All day Reckless had been lucky. But the enemy fire was fierce. Late in the afternoon someone yelled, "They've got Reckless!" She was half way up the hill and blood was pouring down her face. She just kept plodding toward the guns.

Lieutenant Pedersen came running. He wiped the blood from her face and sighed with relief. The cut was long but

shallow. Quickly the men unloaded the shells. Then Reckless turned and started down the hill again.

Later she was hit in the side. But that didn't stop her either. She just kept going until the battle was finally won.

Reckless was so tired now she could hardly walk. She stumbled again and again as Sergeant Latham led her back to camp. Once more he offered her some oats. But she was too tired to eat. Quickly he rubbed the dust and sweat from her body. He covered her with a blanket. And he patted her gently as she fell asleep on her feet.

Later one of the Marines added up the things Reckless had done during the battle for Outpost Vegas. She had made fifty-one trips to the guns — *forty-six of them by herself.* She had carried more than 9,000 pounds of shells on her back. She had run and then walked and finally crept more than thirty-five miles through a storm of enemy fire — and been wounded twice. But nothing had been able to stop her from doing her job.

Many Marines knew and loved Reckless before the battle for Outpost Vegas. Now she became a real Marine Corps heroine. One man who grew to love Reckless was Marine Corps General Randolph Pate. General Pate visited Reckless whenever he could. He called her "that lovely little lady, Reckless."

Soldiers are often honored for their bravery in battle. Reckless's friends thought she should be honored too. So one warm spring day Reckless was led out onto a big field crowded with her Marine Corps friends.

She was wearing a beautiful red silk blanket that the men of the Reckless Rifles had bought. (Half way across the field she tried to eat a corner of it, but someone stopped her in time.)

Reckless was led up to a platform. An officer stepped forward. Everyone grew

silent as he read: "Reckless has per-
formed the duties of ammunition car-
rier in a superb manner. Her disregard
for her own safety under fire was an in-
spiration to troops everywhere . . ."

Now it was General Pate's turn to
honor Reckless. He pinned a special set
of bars to her blanket.

She was *Sergeant* Reckless now.

THE STORY OF CLEVER HANS

the horse who knew all the answers

Hans lived with his master in Berlin, Germany. One day Mr. von Osten invited some friends to his house. He led them to a courtyard where the horse was waiting quietly. "Are you ready, Hans?" he asked.

And the horse nodded!

"How much is four plus three?" Mr. von Osten asked. Hans raised his right foreleg and began to tap his hoof on the old stone floor of the courtyard. "One, two, three," he tapped, "four, five, six, seven" — and stopped.

Everyone began to talk at once. Mr. von Osten just smiled — and asked another question.

"It's twelve-thirty now," he said to the horse. "How many minutes must pass before it will be one o'clock?" Quickly Hans tapped *thirty*.

Next Mr. von Osten spread out six squares of cloth. Each was a different color. "Pick up the green one," he ordered. Hans walked over and stopped in front of the green square. He picked it up in his teeth and carried it back to his master.

Then Mr. von Osten looked around at his friends. "There is a lady here," he told Hans, "who is wearing a hat with pink flowers on it. Will you point her

out for the rest of us?" The woman was
small — and she was standing behind
several other people. But Hans found
her just the same.

For the next hour Mr. von Osten
asked questions — and Hans answered
them. He was right almost every time.

Finally Mr. von Osten said, "That's
enough for today. But Hans will be here
tomorrow to answer more questions."

All this happened about seventy-five
years ago. There was no radio or television. Slowly word of the horse and what

he could do spread through Berlin, then all of Germany — and at last into other countries. More and more people came to the von Osten courtyard to see the wonder horse perform.

Clever Hans never disappointed his audiences. He could solve hard arithmetic problems. "How much is nine times sixty-eight?" Mr. von Osten once asked Hans. It took the horse quite a while to tap the right answer — 612!

Almost every day Hans showed his eager audiences some new talent. He could tell all sorts of things apart — even if they were almost the same size or shade or shape. Hans could also give the right answer when asked the time. And the days and weeks and months of the year.

One day Mr. von Osten stretched a rope across the courtyard. On the rope he hung a number of cards. On each card a word was printed. "Where is the card that says 'hello'?" he asked. Hans walked up to the HELLO card and nudged it with his nose. "And which card says 'Germany'?" Hans picked the correct card again. Finally Mr. von Osten asked, "And which is your own special card?" Hans walked up to the card that said HANS and gave it a really hard nudge.

"The only thing that horse can't do is talk," one man said. But other people said Hans did that too — with his hoof.

Hans had one talent that amazed people more than all the rest. Mr. von Osten could stand in front of the horse and just *think* of a question. He didn't move his lips or make the slightest sound. Yet Hans would answer the question anyway. So Clever Hans could read his master's mind too!

But not everyone agreed that Hans was a real thinking horse. Paul Bushe had worked with circus animals nearly all his life. "I know all the tricks," he bragged. "Nobody can fool me — no matter how smart he thinks he is." He thought Mr. von Osten was sending

Hans signals — signals that told the horse exactly what to do.

Mr. Bushe wanted to find those hidden signals. So he paid a surprise visit to the von Osten courtyard. With him were five other men. He told Mr. von Osten that they were there to study him while he worked with Hans. One man would stare at his head. Another would watch his left arm. A third would watch his right. The last two men would watch one leg each.

Mr. von Osten nodded grimly. He knew that the circus trainer was calling him a liar and a cheat to his face. "And what will *you* watch?" he asked.

"Oh, *I* shall watch *everything*," Paul Bushe answered grandly.

Mr. von Osten began asking questions — and Hans as usual answered most of them correctly. All the while the six men watched. They watched so hard one man said he almost forgot to breathe.

Finally Mr. Bushe threw up his

hands. "Forgive me," he said to Mr. von Osten. "I still find it hard to believe... but I was wrong. No signals have passed between you and the horse. Not a one. I am the greatest circus trainer in Germany — and I am going to tell the world that Clever Hans is indeed a thinking horse. As a matter of fact, he can think better than most people I know!"

A few weeks later another man came to Mr. von Osten's courtyard. Carl Shillings was a famous explorer. For many years he had lived in faraway lands. "I have never seen Clever Hans — and he's never seen me," he said to Mr. von Osten. "There is no way I could have worked out to send him signals. Will you let *me* question the horse?"

"Of course I will," Mr. von Osten said. "I will even leave the courtyard if you wish. Then you can work with Hans all by yourself."

As soon as he was alone Mr. Shillings began to ask Hans questions. At first the horse seemed confused. He pranced a little and looked around the courtyard. But soon he settled down and began to answer Mr. Shillings's questions.

He made a few mistakes, but before long he was giving one right answer after another. So a perfect stranger could ask Hans questions too — a man who could not possibly be part of any plan to fool people. Surely this was final proof that Clever Hans was a true thinking horse!

But still a few people had questions. One of these was a scientist named Oskar Pfungst. Other people had studied Hans for a few hours, or a few days. Professor Pfungst decided he would work for as long as it took to finally solve the mystery of Clever Hans.

First Professor Pfungst started out asking questions, just as other people had done. And Hans answered easily. Then one day the scientist thought of something new. He asked Hans a question that was different in one important

way from all the other questions the big horse had ever been asked. He asked the horse a question *he didn't know the answer to himself.* "How far is it from Berlin to London, England?" he asked.

Poor Hans! He tried again and again to answer that question. But he couldn't do it. The Professor grew more and more excited. He kept asking questions. When he asked a question he knew the answer to, Hans knew the answer. When he asked a question that he didn't know the answer to, Hans didn't either.

Before the day was over, Professor Pfungst knew that Hans couldn't really add or subtract or multiply or divide. He couldn't tell colors or coins or playing cards apart. He couldn't read or tell the time. Hans wasn't a thinking horse at all. He only "knew" as much as the person who was questioning him — and no more!

That meant that the person questioning Hans *was* signaling him. But how? Even the Professor himself must be sending signals — but he had no idea how he was doing it.

Day after day Professor Pfungst continued to ask Hans questions. He watched as many other people questioned the horse. And little by little he began to understand.

Most trained animals can follow signals — like a hand movement or a change in the tone of voice. But none of these planned signals had ever been used with Hans. No, Professor Pfungst announced, people who questioned Hans were signaling Hans even though they did not mean to.

First the person asked Hans a question — and naturally he grew a little tense, a little nervous, as he waited for the horse's answer. When this happened many tiny body changes began to take place — changes the person wasn't trying to make at all. A muscle might quiver in his ear. He might swallow a few more times than usual. His lips might tighten. Or one of his eyebrows would give the slightest twitch. All these were signs of tension. And these signs told Hans to start giving his answer.

Suppose the person had asked Hans how much five plus five is. With each tap of Hans's hoof, the person got more and more tense. $1-2-3-4-5-6-7-8-9-$ Then, as Hans tapped 10, the person relaxed.

Now another whole group of tiny changes began to take place. The person might take a slightly deeper breath — or begin to breathe more slowly. His lips might open a little. His eyelids might droop. His skin might even grow a bit pinker. All these are tiny signs of relaxation. And put together they told Hans to stop.

When someone wanted Hans to nod *yes,* he couldn't help making some kind of upward motion himself. And when someone wanted Hans to walk over to something — a person or perhaps a colored cloth or ball — he couldn't help making some small movement in that direction. Hans would wander around until he happened to pass in front of what the person was thinking about. Then the person would relax — and Hans would stop. He had given the "right" answer again.

So Clever Hans couldn't really think — not the way people do. Yet he was still a very special horse. He had puzzled one expert after another for a long, long while. He might not have been able to read minds — but there was no doubt about it. He was one of the champion *muscle* readers of all time!

BIBLIOGRAPHY

Brookshier, Frank. *The Burro*. Oklahoma: University of Oklahoma Press, 1974.

Casey, Brigid, and Lavine, Sigmund. *Wonders of the World of Horses*. New York: Dodd, Mead & Company, 1972.

Clabby, John. *The Natural History of the Horse*. New York: Taplinger Publishing Company, Inc., 1976.

Darling, Lois and Louis. *Sixty Million Years of Horses*. New York: William Morrow and Company, 1960.

Dobie, J. Frank. *Mustangs and Cow Horses*. Texas: Southern Methodist University Press.

Dobie, J. Frank. *The Mustangs*. New York: Curtis Publishing Company, 1934.

Felton, Harold W. *A Horse Named Justin Morgan*. New York: Dodd, Mead & Company, 1962.

Geer, Andrew. *Reckless, Pride of the Marines*. New York: E. P. Dutton and Company, Inc., 1955.

Henry, Marguerite. *Brighty of Grand Canyon*. Chicago: Rand McNally & Company, 1953.

Henry, Marguerite. *Misty of Chincoteague*. Chicago: Rand McNally & Company, 1947.

Hunt, Frazier and Hunt, Robert. *Horses and Heroes: The Story of the Horse in America for 450 Years.* New York: Charles Scribner's Sons, 1949.

May, Julian. *Horses, How They Came To Be.* New York: Holiday House, 1968.

Pfungst, Oskar. *Clever Hans.* New York: Henry Holt and Company, 1911.

Runnquist, Ake (edited by). *Horses in Fact and Fiction.* London: Johnathan Cape, 1957.

Russell, George B. *Hoofprints in Time.* New York: Barnes and Company, Inc., 1966.

Savitt, Sam. *True Horse Stories.* New York: Dodd, Mead and Company, 1970.

Simpson, George G. *Horses.* New York: Oxford University Press, 1951.

Ticknor, Caroline. *The Book of Famous Horses.* Boston: Houghton Mifflin Company, 1929.

Vischer, Peter. *Horses and Horsemen.* London: D. Van Nostrand Company, 1967.

Wade, Horace. *Tales of the Turf.* New York: Vantage Press, 1956.

Wilding, Suzanne. *Horses in Action.* New York: St. Martin's Press, 1972.

MAGAZINES

"Abilities of an Educated Horse." *Popular Science Monthly,* February, 1913, pp. 168–76.

"Brighty, Free Citizen." *Sunset Magazine,* August 1922, pp. 70–71.

"Fable of the Thinking Horse." *Review of Reviews,* November, 1910, pp. 606–7.

"Frisky Son for Misty." *Life Magazine,* May 23, 1960, pp. 67–8+.

"Goodbye to the Wild Horse." *Reader's Digest*, May, 1971, pp. 227–30+.

"Hans, the Wonderful Orloff Stallion." *McClure's Magazine*, May, 1905, pp. 84–92.

"Horse Sense Extraordinary." *Literary Digest*, March 22, 1913, pp. 663–4.

"Misty Goes Back Home." *Life Magazine*, June 10, 1957, pp. 63–4+.

"Mustangs." *Life Magazine*, January 17, 1969, pp. 42–54.

"Quick Trick Mathematics." *Literary Digest.* May 10, 1913, pp. 1058–9.

"Reasoning Horse." *Scientific American.* September 24, 1904, p. 213.

"Reckless, Pride of the Marines." *Saturday Evening Post*, April 17, 1954, pp. 31+.

Red Carpet for Sergeant Reckless." *Saturday Evening Post*, October 22, 1955, pp. 22–3+.

"Reporter At Large: Hunting Mustangs." *New Yorker Magazine*, April 10, 1954, pp. 66+.

"Tales of the Turf." *Saturday Evening Post*, June 5, 1926, pp. 54–8.

"Talking Horse." *New Yorker Magazine,* October 13, 1945, pp. 80–90.

"The Mystery of Clever Hans." *Literary Digest*, February 6, 1915.

"The Pacing White Mustang." *American Mercury Magazine*, December, 1927, pp. 435–42.

"The Passing of Brighty." *Outing Magazine*, February 23, 1928, p. 225.

"The Story of the Horse." *National Geographic Magazine*, May, 1923, pp. 455–566.

"Tiny Horse Opera For Youngsters: Misty, the Chincoteague Colt." *Life Magazine*, May 26, 1961, pp. 65–6+.

INDEX